CAREERS IN THE REAL ESTATE BUSINESS

SALES – BROKER/AGENT

REAL ESTATE DEVELOPMENT

TO SAY THAT CAREERS IN REAL ESTATE are critical to the functioning of society would be a gross understatement. Nobody can do much of anything without land. Without it, where would you put your stuff? Or yourself? Even the phrase "real estate" is rooted in the idea that land and buildings are fundamentally different from anything else in a person's estate, or sum total of their wealth. Other forms of property can be quickly and easily converted into other things: Stocks can be sold, cash can be used to buy things. Land and buildings are more permanent. Land is an extremely valuable commodity. As real estate agents like to say, "You know what they say about land: They're not making any more of it."

There are many careers directly involved in real estate. This report will concentrate on real estate agents who buy and sell commercial and residential real estate, usually on behalf of clients. It will also look into closely related professions like real-estate development, which is the natural by-product of buying and selling property, and often undertaken by the same people and businesses.

Real estate is also a classic entrepreneurial business. Most real estate agents are technically self-employed and pay a fee to be associated with a realty company.

Read on and you will learn how to get some experience right away, what to study in school, how much money you may make at various points in your career and what you may like most about the career and even what you may not like.

WHAT YOU CAN DO NOW

YOU CAN GET A GOOD GRIP ON THE real estate business right now. Have a long talk with people you know about real estate. Everybody who has ever bought or rented a property has an opinion about real estate. People who have moved around a few times or whose businesses are especially dependent upon real estate will have many varying opinions.

It has been said that the first rule of real estate is "location, location, location." This means that, ultimately, a piece of property is in the right place for a prospective buyer or renter, or it isn't.

Buying real estate is a complex process that takes considerable time and requires careful attention to detail. Most homeowners remember even minor details of their real estate adventures, from negotiating over prices to finding the best interest rate, and deciding which renovations needed to be made immediately and which could wait.

The Internet has fundamentally altered the real estate business. Anybody with Internet access can peruse real estate listings from all over the world, looking at photographs, comparing neighborhoods, and dreaming big dreams. The best real estate sites, like Trulia and Zillow, host thousands of listings at any given time and offer a huge amount of related information, like local crime statistics, ratings of school districts, locations of amenities like restaurants and grocery stores. Follow a few individual properties and see what you can learn.

Read books about real estate. There are hundreds of recent editions to choose from. Pick a few covering a range of related areas, including how to buy a house, how to sell a house, and how to renovate a house. Look into your local housing codes and zoning ordinances. These are the laws that govern what can be done with land and buildings in your area. All of these topics are important to success in real estate.

HISTORY OF THE CAREER

REAL ESTATE IS A YOUNG BUSINESS, AT least in the modern sense. What we think of as "real estate" is the product of thousands of years of social and economic evolution. Real estate is still evolving, and probably always will.

There was no concept of land ownership for most of human history because people had to move constantly in order to find food. Pre-agrarian societies did not know how to plant crops or raise animals, so they formed into small bands or tribes and followed the seasons and herds wherever they led. These are called hunter-gatherer societies. People did not stay in one place and claim that the land was theirs alone.

This changed about 10,000 years ago when the first tribes discovered how to grow basic crops like wheat and corn. For the first time there was reason to settle down and own a piece of land. Staying in one place was not only easier than being constantly on the move, it was liberating. Some people could be freed from the routine of hunting and gathering so they could do other jobs in the community. These planted societies are known as agrarian societies.

As soon as people stopped moving around, land became valuable. It was necessary for farming, for homes, and for businesses. As societies became more efficient and productive, land became the basis for entire civilizations. Powerful leaders established the first nations and exercised their authority in part by determining who could own or use the land under their control, creating an aristocracy. This is the basis of the system known as feudalism, where a powerful landlord rents small parcels of property to people who pay taxes to the landlord in return for protection and other services. In most feudal societies only a handful of people are legally allowed to own the land.

The slow evolution of a merchant class of businesspeople whose wealth rivaled that of the aristocracy changed the relationship between people and land. In most modern societies anybody can own land as long as they can pay for it. Still, land has always been treated differently from other things people own. Land ownership is always registered with the local government jurisdiction. Rules and regulations, taxes, environmental limitations, and zoning codes can be onerous, and they are strictly enforced.

The complexity and importance of land use gave rise to the earliest real estate agents. Baird & Warner, the first real estate agency in the United States, was founded in Chicago in 1855 to capitalize upon the rapid growth of the city. The company helped newcomers to find the land they needed to build homes, factories and offices. Other firms soon followed suit in other markets. The National Association of Realtors was founded in 1908, also in Chicago, as the National Association of Real Estate Exchanges.

By the 1920s, real estate was a well-established profession. Professionalizing the process of real estate sales was the first step toward creating the modern real estate business we know today.

Property sales are bound by many laws and regulations, making real estate transactions very difficult for people not trained in the process. Nevertheless, some homeowners do choose to sell their property themselves. They list their property for sale "by owner" and figure out how to navigate the complex legal and financial process by themselves. Some buyers choose to handle purchases on their own too.

Most buyers and sellers hire agents to act on their behalf simply because the process is so daunting. States adopted licensing and education regulations in order to make sure that real estate agents know what they are doing and that they understand the ethical issues involved in negotiating on behalf of another person.

Multiple listing services have been around since the 1800s,

first in the form of handshake deals among real estate brokers to help each other buy and sell property, and then as formalized networks that are open only to brokers and their agents. Access to a multiple listing service – commonly known as an MLS – is still one of the most important advantages agents receive when they sign on with a brokerage. Current prices, price history, ownership records, number of days on the market, and neighborhood statistics are just some of the important data points in listing records.

There is no single MLS in the United States. There are more than 800 of them, all privately owned. The advent of easy-to-search Internet-based MLSs in the 1990s was one of the greatest leaps in the history of the real estate business.

Today's real estate business is one of the key industries that make the American economy flourish. Ups and downs in the real estate market track the fluctuations in the overall economy. Rising real estate prices generally mean that the overall economy is heading up, while falling prices indicate a decline. For millions of people the real estate they own represents the largest portion of their net worth, and maybe their life's savings. Thousands of dedicated professionals keep the business running, protecting the interests of their clients.

WHERE YOU WILL WORK

THERE ARE REAL ESTATE CAREERS TO pursue anywhere there is land. There is a real estate professional just about everywhere with an interest in helping people to buy, sell, and rent land, buildings, and dwellings of all kinds. Some markets are busier than others, and specific types of real estate, like condominiums or single-family houses, heavily characterize some locations.

Some real estate markets are extremely specialized.

Manhattan, the borough most people think of when they think of New York City, is characterized almost entirely by condominiums (apartments that people own rather than rent) and office space. A relatively small percentage of real estate sales in New York are of entire buildings, from townhouses to skyscrapers. There are very few yards in Manhattan, and most of the grass is in tiny plots planted on rooftops. Property values in Manhattan are stratospherically high, with modest condominiums selling for millions of dollars. This is a very specialized, very upscale market that requires extremely specific local knowledge and outstanding customer service skills. People in the market for a $5 million condominium do not do business with amateurs.

On the other hand, many areas in the West and Midwest are characterized by wide-open spaces and land zoned for agricultural and industrial use. Residential real estate in these communities tends to be relatively inexpensive single-family houses, usually with large yards, garages and driveways. Many areas have been deemed conservation areas or are subject to environmental laws that govern what they can and cannot be used for. This requires very different real estate knowledge than selling pricey condominiums in New York City.

Most parts of the United States offer fairly diverse real estate markets consisting of residential and commercial real estate. Most real estate agents specialize in either residential or commercial real estate, and some may further specialize in specific types of real estate, geographic areas, or even specific city neighborhoods. Real estate agents are licensed by states and can generally practice anywhere in the state or states in which they hold a license.

Specializing in an area or type of real estate allows real estate agents to develop targeted professional expertise. As you research career opportunities in real estate you should look into all the options and determine what suits you best.

Many people use the terms "real estate agent" and "realtor" interchangeably. Actually, the word "Realtor" – note the upper case – is a trademark owned by the National Association of Realtors (NAR), the largest trade association in the real estate industry. Only real estate agents who belong to the NAR are entitled to call themselves Realtors. So all Realtors are real estate agents, but not all real estate agents are Realtors. Unless referring specifically to Realtors, this report will use the term "real estate agent" or simply "agent" to describe a professional involved in buying or selling real estate.

YOUR WORK DUTIES

Real Estate Agent

When most people think of real estate professionals they think of real estate agents. That is because real estate agents are the front line of the real estate business, and anybody who has purchased a home or commercial real estate has probably dealt with one. They are the dedicated professionals who squire clients from one property to the next, provide good advice and never lose their cheerful demeanor.

Real estate agents are licensed to assist clients with buying and selling property. They work for brokers or brokerages (a real estate firm owned by a broker or brokers), and provide the customer service necessary to make the transaction go smoothly. Agents can spend months working with clients to find for them the property that fits their needs. Sometimes the process goes smoothly but it can also get very complicated. Many buyers do not really know what they want and may use up much of their agent's valuable time driving from one property to the next. Some clients are only available in the evenings and on weekends, making it difficult for agents to spend time with   their own families. Clients can be extraordinarily fussy, dismissing potential properties for trivial things like doorknobs or paint colors, both of which are easily changed. This is where agents earn their commissions. Some clients really are hard-to-please, but most just do not know enough about the process to make decisions without help. That is why they use agents.

Agents are expected to have a basic knowledge of home construction, plumbing, electrical, landscaping, building codes, local schools, crime statistics, neighborhood associations, the state of the property market, banking and lending, kitchen and bathroom design, cable and Internet providers, and anything else a client wants to know. Agents also need to attend to many other duties, like advertising, preparing contracts, getting new listings they can sell and posting them on an MLS, meeting with potential clients, and promoting their own business.

Real Estate Broker

Real estate brokers are often indistinguishable from real estate agents. The main difference is in the licensing. Brokers are licensed to own or manage brokerages that employ real estate agents. All real estate transactions end with a broker, even if the parties involved have dealt only with agents up to that point.

Many brokers work in the field just like agents, and perform all the same functions. Many others spend most of their time in the office managing their business. Still others do both, and attend to both clients and managerial duties.

Managing a business requires certain skills. Most agents are self-employed and need to manage their own affairs, but managing a complex business with office space, employees and overhead requires a much broader range of abilities. Brokers typically handle marketing and promotions for their firm, usually affiliated with a nationally known company which provides brand recognition, advertising, and additional services. Brokers must also be conversant in basic business accounting, taxation, law, and finance.

Real Estate Appraisers and Assessors

Determining the value of real estate can be a complex process. Supply and demand determines the final price of a piece of real estate, but appraisers give all parties a place to start negotiations. Assessors perform a similar function, but usually to determine the value of a property for tax purposes.

Appraisers prepare detailed reports on the properties they appraise, using multiple criteria to determine their value. They inspect properties and take note of characteristics that will have an impact on property value. They document properties by taking photographs and measurements. They also research nearby properties in order to get a picture of property values in the same neighborhood and to find properties that are roughly comparable in size, location, amenities and condition to the property they are appraising. These are called comps. Comps are often cited by agents and their clients when negotiating the final price for a piece of property.

Appraisers tend to specialize in one type of property. Some specialize in commercial or residential, while others take the distinctions a step further and zero in on condominiums or office space, for example. Appraisers can work for themselves or for firms specializing in real estate services.

Assessors also determine property values but for tax purposes. They work for local governments, like cities or townships, and apply complex formulas to properties to determine their taxable value. Whereas appraisers tend to work on one property at a time, assessors may value entire blocks or even whole neighborhoods in order to make sure that everybody in a given area is paying similar taxes. Every jurisdiction uses its own formula in generating property tax assessments. Generally, they take into account the size of the property and its location. Then a tax rate is applied to the resulting valuation, and the owner's annual tax is determined. In most jurisdictions property owners are entitled to appeal the assessor's findings if they think their taxes are too high. Some jurisdictions, like the state of California, have eliminated traditional assessments in favor of simpler formulas like a percentage of the most recent sales price.

Home Inspector

Home inspectors do not determine the value of a home, but their inspection reports can have a great deal of influence on the purchase price. Home inspectors take stock of the physical condition of homes for sale, inspecting the material state of the structure and its associated systems, like plumbing, electrical and gas hookups. They consider aspects like the age of the roof and whether the basement leaks.

Home inspections are a prudent choice before buying a home, and may be required by the lending institutions involved in the transaction. Home inspections are typically performed after a buyer and seller have entered into a contract, but before the sale is closed and made permanent. A home inspection contingency is a common clause in contracts between buyers and sellers. If a home inspection reveals a serious issue in the house, like potentially dangerous electrical problems or a cracked foundation that will cost a fortune to repaid, buyers can either back out of the contract without penalty or negotiate a monetary solution to the problem. Sometimes sellers agree to reduce the price of their property, sometimes they agree to fix the problem before the transaction is closed.

Home inspectors must be licensed, and licensing requirements vary among jurisdictions. There are many training programs available to satisfy the licensing requirements. Many home inspectors are self-employed and develop strong relationships with agents and brokers in their areas so that they will get the call when a client needs an inspection.

Property Manager

Property managers take care of properties for other people. Some companies are devoted solely to property management, and many real estate brokerages run property management operations as an associated business.

Property managers can run anything from office buildings, to apartment complexes, to single-family houses and condominiums. Managers may or may not be directly involved in buying or selling property. A property manager in charge of a condominium complex takes care of the common spaces like hallways and swimming pools and sees to general maintenance of the complex. Office building managers perform the same function for commercial spaces. Individual property owners often hire property managers to take care of their properties when they move away or put their properties up for rent. Property managers serve as landlords, screening tenants, collecting rent and being the go-to person for repairs and maintenance. Most states require property managers to be licensed agents or brokers, or to earn a property management license.

Real Estate Investor

Real estate investor is a very broad term that could apply to anybody from a person who owns an apartment for rent, all the way to billionaire real estate investor Donald Trump. You do not need to have a full-time career as a real estate investor in order to do some investing occasionally. You might be surprised at how many people own income-producing real estate. If you get into the real estate business and learn the ins and outs of making money in real estate, you will probably want to try your hand at investing, even if only on a small scale.

Commonly known as "income property," real estate that generates cash flow is one of the best investments around. For example, you buy a condominium for $250,000. With a 20-percent down payment and an interest rate of 4.5

percent, your monthly mortgage payment will be about $1,000. Add a homeowner's association fee, taxes and insurance, and your total monthly bill may come to about $1,500. If you can rent that condominium for $1,800 per month you will earn $3,600 per year in additional income. If you hang onto the property for 10 years and never raise the rent (which you probably will) you will make $36,000. If the value of the property increases by 30 percent over the decade, to $325,000, you could sell it for a profit of $75,000. That amounts to $111,000 in total income. If you own multiple properties – just do the math.

STORIES OF REAL ESTATE PROFESSIONALS

I Own a Real Estate Brokerage

"I own a busy real estate brokerage in a major metropolitan area. We specialize in residential real estate and have helped clients to buy and sell everything from tiny condos to enormous mansions. We have a major presence in our market. You will see our signs on lawns all over town.

I majored in business administration in college. I wasn't sure what I wanted to do with it, but I knew I wanted to be in business. I held several positions in marketing and management before deciding that I needed to do something on my own. Real estate looked like the ticket. Like most people in real estate, I got into this business as an agent. I liked the flexibility and the ability to make serious money based solely on my own efforts. I also appreciated the opportunity to get involved in the community and get to know lots of people. No business is more local than real estate. It's one of the things I still love about my career.

I did pretty well as an agent and decided I wanted to become a broker. Brokers do all the same things agents do, but they can also complete transactions, and own and manage brokerages. Every state has slightly different licensing requirements but the gist of all of them is that agents help people buy and sell properties, but the deal has to go through a licensed broker. As soon as I passed the tests and had my broker's license in hand, I moved to a new brokerage as a manager. After a few years of working for somebody else I opened my own brokerage.

Being in charge is completely different from being an agent. I work regular hours, for one thing. More than that, I am responsible for everything that happens here – legally, financially and ethically. My real estate functions, like overseeing transactions, are only part of the job. Mostly, I'm a boss like any other small business owner. I have to run the business. I hire and fire people. I manage training programs, look after the accounting and finance, and maintain relations with our corporate affiliate.

The corporate affiliate is one of the most important parts of running a real estate brokerage. Most brokerages are affiliated with a larger company through a franchise. I own my brokerage but I do not own the brand name and the logo that goes on my signs. Those familiar branding elements are owned by a much larger corporation. This association gives me instant brand recognition in the form of a nationwide real estate company. The company also provides me with cooperative promotions, market research, training and education for my team, and important business tools like special computer programs and access to the company's private listings. Buying a franchise was one of the smartest things I've ever done. It gives my business a solid framework and reputation.

I'd recommend this career to anybody who loves the real estate business and who really wants to take charge. Being the boss comes with perks, but it also comes with great responsibility. Accounting chores can be a pain. Nobody likes to fire people. Sometimes the corporate affiliate makes demands that are tough to meet. It's all part of what it means to be the boss. Some days I'd like to go back to being an agent. Most days, however, I'm happy to be right where I am."

I Am a Residential Real Estate Agent

"You don't want to know how many miles I put on my car in a typical year. I spend roughly half of every day driving clients from one house to the next, trying to find the home of their dreams. But I do more than just drive – I advise.

Advice and consultation are really my primary functions. Buyers and sellers don't really need agents, not legally. They need us to help guide them through the complex process of buying or selling property. You would be amazed at the things that clients expect me to know about. Of course, I should know about the state of the local property market and related issues like schools and crime. I am also expected to be an expert in matching doorknobs to a specific architectural style. Choosing the right species of grass for sun or shade. Predicting commuting times from one location to another at every time of day. These are only a few of the questions I am asked.

At first I was surprised by how much my clients expected me to know, but it quickly became one of the best parts of the job. I have an easy excuse to delve into everything even loosely related to real estate, like local politics, architecture, gardening, education, transportation and interior design.

Knowing a little bit about many things is a good fit for a liberal-arts college graduate. I majored in English in college, which is what many students do when they don't know what they want to do with their lives. I started out as a journalist working for local newspapers, which is another job that encourages learning something about many different things. Then parenting took over, and I didn't work outside the home for a few years. When my kids got a little older I wanted to do something that didn't require working regular hours but offered the possibility of making real money. That's when I decided to become a real estate agent.

My kids don't need as much of my attention as they used to, but I still appreciate the flexibility offered by this career. I've also established my reputation in this market, so my earnings continue to grow, even though I don't work anything like 9 to 5.

There are only two things I dislike about this job. The first are clients who don't know what they're looking for. Everybody wants to look around a bit, and that's fine. But indecisive clients who go back and forth from condos in the city to houses in the suburbs, or horse farms in the country, drive me a bit batty. I maintain my professionalism, of course, but those clients can get tiresome.

I'm often out with clients in the evenings and on weekends when I would rather be spending time with my family. But didn't I say that I wanted a job that didn't require working regular hours? Welcome to the life of a real estate agent."

I Am a Property Manager

I am a licensed real estate agent but I spend most of my time running a small property management business. I manage rental properties for private owners and corporations. My company is actually part of a real estate brokerage. We are a full-service brokerage and help clients buy and sell commercial and residential real estate. We also manage commercial and residential property. I run the residential part of the property management business.

Whether the apartment units are owned or rented, there are huge common areas like gyms, swimming pools, hallways, lobbies, roof decks, and grounds that need to be taken care of. My management company does all that.

In rental apartment buildings we also show prospective tenants around the building, run credit checks and handle leases. We have contracts with many large buildings in our metro area. We also provide services to private property owners who need somebody to look after their property. Many people own income-producing property. Some manage their property themselves, but most hire professionals like us. We charge a fee every month but we also save landlords a lot of hassles.

We also make it possible for people to rent their properties when they have to move away and don't want to sell their property. We have a large roster of military families who fall into this category. They buy homes they want to move into when they leave active duty but need somebody to manage them for a few years until they can come home.

Property management is an interesting part of the real estate business. I was an agent for many years before I was offered this job. I still do some property sales but I really enjoy management. I can see why brokerages offer property management services. The business keeps the brokerage's name in the public eye. Our agents are clearly well represented at the condo buildings we manage because our name is everywhere. There is a clear linkage between buying and selling property, and managing it. Big apartment buildings sometimes change hands, just like houses. When one of our buildings goes up for sale, who do you think gets the listing?"

I Am a Home Inspector

"Nobody should buy or sell property without getting a home inspection. Unless you're an expert in property construction and code-enforcement issues you have no way of knowing what might be wrong with the property you're about to buy or sell. People who skip inspections can have some nasty surprises.

I got into this business after years of dabbling in real estate as an investor. I bought houses, fixed them up and sold them for a profit. This practice is commonly known as flipping, and it's a fun and interesting way to make money. Along the way, I hired a number of home inspectors and saw just about everything. Cracked foundations, plumbing and electrical that wasn't up to code or was just plain dangerous, holes in roofs, insect infestations, lead-based paint, broken windows, wood rot, and you-name-it. So I decided to earn a license to become a home inspector.

Every state's licensing requirements are different, but in my state I had to go through a comprehensive classroom-training program and then work for an inspector in the field for several months. I was lucky in that I already knew a lot from my experience flipping houses, but it was still a challenging process.

I get calls from banks, real estate agents, and people looking to buy or sell property. For a typical single-family house, I spend about three hours going through every nook and cranny looking for trouble spots. Electrical and foundation problems are the most common. Old houses were often wired with a system known as knob-and-tube wiring that can fray and expose live wires. Most building codes require knob-and-tube to be replaced whenever major changes are made to the house. People just want to know how much of this there is in the house before they buy it in case they want to spend the money to replace it. As to foundations, they can crack in ways that most people would never notice until it's too late. Foundations can be extremely expensive to fix if they are neglected for too long.

When I'm done, I write up a report and generally give it to both parties. Big problems have to be dealt with one way or another. Sometimes sellers agree to reduce their price, other times they just fix the problem before the sale is completed. Many sales are called off after inspections turn up problems that nobody wants to solve. I play an important role in the real estate business. I'd recommend this job to anybody."

I Am a Commercial Real Estate Broker

"Commercial real estate is entirely different from residential real estate. Most jurisdictions don't make any legal distinctions between the two, and licensed brokers and agents can work with either, but that's where the similarity ends.

Commercial real estate is not a part-time, flexible job. The people who buy and sell commercial real estate do so during regular working hours. That's when they need my assistance. My clients tend to wear suits, so I do I too. They know what they want and value their time very highly. I don't spend months driving my clients all over town.

I specialize in office space in a major city. My turf tends to be downtown and a few neighborhoods on the edge that attract small and large service businesses that need a lot of desk space for their employees. I have colleagues who specialize in other types of commercial real estate, like industrial property, warehouses, restaurants, and retail space.

Locating exactly the perfect office space can be a very complex equation. Many businesses need to be as close to their customers as possible. That's why accounting firms like downtown office space near the big business headquarters offices. Businesses value their address, too. Simply being on the right street enhances their prestige and helps them to get customers. The practical issues like square footage and access to parking usually come up after getting the general location right. My clients know what they need and count on me to help them find it.

I have a Master of Business Administration degree in finance with a concentration in real estate. The degree doesn't just help me do my job, it helps me to speak my clients' language. They are businesspeople. My credibility goes up when it's apparent that I am operating on their level.

I handle every aspect of commercial real estate transactions, from finding clients and properties to handling all of the paperwork and legal process. I am a licensed broker, so I can legally complete transactions. I am a partner in a large brokerage, which gives me access to in-house expertise and every kind of business service. We are a major company in our own right. In fact, we're growing so quickly that we outgrew our old offices. So I found us a new space, on a prestigious street not far from some of our biggest clients. Right where we belong."

PERSONAL QUALIFICATIONS

BEING A SUCCESSFUL REAL ESTATE agent requires a combination of customer service skills, diplomacy and uncommon professionalism.

Good customer service is one of those things that is hard to define but easy to recognize. Restaurant servers and retail clerks need excellent customer service skills. Generally speaking, however, they do not deal with transactions that take months and involve their customers' life savings. It is very common for real estate agents to work with clients for months or even years to buy or sell property. Some agents have informal, handshake deals with certain clients to buy and sell all of their properties. Hundreds of thousands of dollars, or even millions, will change hands along the way.

Do you have the kind of dedication and perseverance necessary to take the same people on house-hunting tours several times a week for months? This is a typical cycle for residential real estate sales. How will you react when a client gets hung up on trivial things like kitchen cabinet doorknobs or the paint color in a bathroom, both of which can be easily changed? How about clients who look at condos in the city and acre lots in the country and can't make up their minds where they really want to live? Or sellers who turn down multiple, reasonable offers and then gripe about the state of the market?

The personal qualities needed by real estate agents go beyond excellent customer service skills and get into the realm of diplomacy. According to the National Association of Realtors, the average price for a single-family house in the United States in a typical recent year was almost $215,000. The average was higher in the Northeast, at almost $270,000, and lower in the Midwest, at about $160,000.

Buyers tend to buy the most expensive home they can afford, while sellers naturally want to maximize the return on their investment. Buying or selling property is something that most people only do a handful of times in their life, maybe only once. This is a very big occasion in anyone's life, and buyers and sellers need to be handled with patience and respect.

The real estate profession is also bound by very strict rules that must be followed at all times. When an agent signs a contract to represent a buyer or seller, that contract is legally and ethically binding. Agents work for their clients, and nobody else. That means that conversations between agents and clients are legally confidential. Agents who break the rules can be subject to professional sanction by the National Association of Realtors or even civil lawsuits. An example of illegal activity would be a buyer's agent telling a seller the top price the buyer would be willing to pay for a property, even if the buyer's current offer is lower. By the same token, an agent working for a seller who tipped off a potential buyer to the seller's lowest acceptable price could face professional sanction or legal action. These negotiations must be conducted at "arm's length," meaning no one can be informed of the private intentions of the other party.

Real estate agents who have been in the business for a long time in the same area tend to get to know one another and develop friendships. Old friends share secrets all the time – but not these secrets. Your professionalism must be unwavering and beyond reproach. Even the slightest hint of impropriety can ruin a reputation, and nobody wants to do business with a disreputable agent.

ATTRACTIVE FEATURES

The income potential is almost unlimited. Ninety percent of American millionaires made their money in real estate. Think about it – 90 percent of all Americans with a net worth of $1 million or more accumulated their wealth by buying, selling or owning real estate – more than all the corporate CEOs and movie star celebrities. Most millionaires are regular people who made good real estate deals. While it may seem like the only way to get rich is through Wall Street or Hollywood, that is not what the statistics say. It is hard to determine the "average" income for real estate professionals because so many choose to work part time, and do not strive for very high earnings, but there is no doubt that the hardest working agents do very well financially.

The majority of people in these careers are self-employed. Rather than work as employees, most agents pay a fee to an established brokerage in exchange for desk space, the right to use the broker's facilities and brand name, and access to the Multiple Listing Service. Most brokerages maintain some kind of performance requirement – usually minimum annual sales – but otherwise let agents run their own business and deal with clients on their own time. Most agents work part time in order to accommodate other obligations, like their families. All agents have to be willing to work odd hours in order to fit the schedules of their clients. This can result in many evenings spent with clients rather than with family, but it can also lead to the flexibility to schedule three-day weekends and never miss a child's theatrical performance, sporting event, or other activity. A career in real estate splits the difference between a full-time job and owing your own business. Agents have the structure and support provided by a brokerage, but the flexibility to manage their own schedules, and choose their own clients.

It is not uncommon for real estate agents to get a little emotional when they complete a sale. Imagine the moment when you hand over the keys to a young couple who have just purchased the home in which they plan to raise a family, or when telling an older couple that the home they have lived in for decades just brought a price that will provide them the retirement of their dreams. Commercial agents take similar satisfaction when they find the right land to expand a business that will create jobs, or when they match a startup company to perfect office space.

UNATTRACTIVE FEATURES

THIS IS A COMPLEX JOB, FILLED WITH legal nuances and requiring a substantial body of knowledge. Real estate careers are not easy and casual. True, many real estate agents work part-time in order to devote time to other parts of their lives. However, do not assume that agents who work 20 to 25 hours per week are slackers. They may have children or other obligations that make real estate a good fit for their busy schedules. That does not make real estate a part-time job. All real estate agents must undergo many hours of accredited professional training and pass a state-mandated exam before they can represent clients. The buying/selling process itself is bewildering, requiring multiple contracts, property inspections, building code inspections, and complex financial arrangements, among other things. Agents are expected to be their clients' primary sources for information on location, school districts, crime statistics, the state of the market and innumerable other issues. Seasoned agents have a huge amount of information at their fingertips. They are also held to a high legal and ethical standard.

Most real estate agents have fairly modest incomes. Just because real estate is the best way to make millions does not mean it will happen without serious effort. You will have to work very hard. The most successful real estate agents will tell you that the secret to success is to treat your career in real estate like a full-time job, no matter how many hours a week you put in. Plunge in and give it everything you have and you will do very well. Like all selling careers, you have to keep trying, never losing your energy and determination to make the sale.

If you have been stuck in a nine-to-five rut for a few years, the thought of working when it suits you can be very tempting. The ability to make your own schedule and not have anybody looking over your shoulder is obviously a plus. Then clients want you to do showings in the evenings or before they go to work in the morning. Then you start getting calls on weekends. You may not have given it much thought yet, but someday you may have children who are booked up with school or work during regular daytime hours and who want to spend time with you in the evenings and on weekends, and that is when you may be your busiest work time. This is a trade-off that comes with all jobs that offer flexible hours.

EDUCATION AND TRAINING

THERE ARE NO FORMAL ACADEMIC requirements to enter the real estate business, although a college degree is highly recommended. Even if you choose not to earn a degree, be aware that this career requires considerable time in the classroom. At a minimum, you will have to study for and pass a state-mandated exam. You will probably want to earn some additional certifications and designations along the way, and they will require diligent study.

Many successful real estate professionals do not have formal academic credentials beyond a high school diploma. They work hard, learn the business, and let their records speak for themselves. They tend to have a great deal of professional training and education, however. They take courses, go to seminars and earn certificates and designations in a wide variety of subjects related to real estate. Many of these certifications and licenses are necessary to legally conduct business or to move up in the world.

A bachelor's degree is required or preferred by some brokerages. A degree will give you an edge on your competitors who do not have degrees, in any case. Many real estate professionals have bachelor's degrees in business administration, marketing or finance. Others have degrees in real estate that combine courses from several disciplines into a curriculum specially designed for students who want to earn a living buying, selling or managing property. You do not have to earn a degree in real estate or business, however. Because many real estate professionals enter the career later in life, they come with a variety of academic backgrounds. Their major is less important than the fact that they earned a degree and are perceived as more well-rounded individuals as a result.

Some real estate professionals earn master's degrees. This is especially true of brokers who own or manage brokerages. Many schools offer master's degrees in real estate, or Master of Business Administration degrees with specialties in real estate or real estate finance. If you plan to become a broker and run a large brokerage with many agents, you may want to earn a graduate degree.

One excellent reason to earn a degree is to set yourself up to complete an internship in real estate. Most internships are full-time jobs related to your major that take the place of classes for a summer or semester. Most internships are paid, and many come with special seminars and other opportunities not available to regular employees. As an intern, you will be able to work alongside established real estate professionals and see how the business works first hand. You may spend most of your time making coffee or running errands, but you will be immersed in the day-to-day operations of the business you think you want to enter. Internships are such a good way to gain real-world knowledge that many colleges and universities require an internship in order to graduate. You will get valuable experience and make connections that will be useful when the time comes to land a full-time job after graduation. Many graduates get their first jobs with the companies where they did their internships.

EARNINGS

MOST REAL ESTATE AGENTS DO WELL, but your earnings will depend almost entirely on your motivation. Real estate agents are paid on commission. They receive a percentage of the sale or purchase price that they helped to negotiate. Commissions are paid to brokers, who then pay their agents an agreed-upon portion of the commission. Commissions tend to be between five and eight percent of the property's purchase price and are split between the brokers on both sides of the transaction, who then make their own arrangements with their agents. Sellers negotiate the commission with their agent before putting their property on the market.

A typical real estate transaction works like this. A property owner hires a broker to list the property. Using the agent's expertise, the property owner agrees to list the property for, say, $300,000 and agrees to a six-percent commission, or $18,000. When the property sells the buyer's broker and the seller's broker split the commission. They can divide the commission any way they want, but even splits are common. So if the property sells for the list price of $300,000, the $18,000 commission is split between the two brokerages. Brokerages then pay their agents a share of the commission. This share varies depending upon the agent's seniority and sales volume, with junior agents earning about 30 to 50 percent of their broker's commission, and senior, high-performing agents earning as much as 75 percent of the commission. In this example, a junior agent working for the seller might earn $2,700, or 30 percent of the $9,000 commission paid to the brokerage, while a senior agent working for the buyer might earn $6,750, or 75 percent of the broker's $9,000 commission.

Residential real estate agents just starting out typically earn about $40,000 to $50,000 annually in their first few years. They spend this time networking, getting to know their territory and putting their name in front of potential clients via websites, cooperative advertising programs with their brokerages, and the time-honored method of placing signs in front yards.

Income can rise rapidly for motivated agents, with annual earnings of $60,000 to $80,000 possible within a few years.

Agents and brokers specializing in commercial real estate generally earn more but they also tend to work in a typical office environment with fairly regular hours and all the demands of a normal job.

Motivated real estate agents can earn more than $100,000 a year, and some earn much more. Motivation is the keyword here. Willingness to put in long hours is part of the equation. Location is another factor. Agents working in Manhattan or Beverly Hills will obviously earn larger commissions on multimillion-dollar sales. But the competition (and cost of living) in such upscale markets is intense, and only the most dedicated survive.

A career in real estate can be a good part-time job, an extremely lucrative full-time one, or something in-between.

OPPORTUNITIES

BECAUSE MOST REAL ESTATE AGENTS and brokers are essentially self-employed, there is never a bad time to enter this profession. Licensing classes are offered year-round. Downturns in the real estate market tend to result in fewer sales and smaller commissions, and veteran agents and brokers with high profiles and long client lists tend to crowd out newcomers when the market gets soft. You can enter the career at any time, but do not expect to cash in big during a down market. Of course, timing of the market and the timing of your life may or may not coincide. If you are ready to get started, get started. Set realistic goals and be patient.

All states require agents and brokers to undergo state-mandated training and pass a test in order to become licensed. You can expand your prospects dramatically by earning additional designations and certifications from the National Association of Realtors. There are dozens of designations and certifications listed on the NAR website – for example, Accredited Land Consultant or Certified International Property Specialist.

Many real estate professionals branch out into property management by becoming a Certified Property Manager. Think you would like to become a General Accredited

Appraiser? The NAR also offers educational programs in subjects like military relocation, and general sales and marketing.

Never forget that the most successful professionals – in any field – make their own opportunities. Real estate is among the few small business ventures that allows you to be creative, pound pavement, and put in long hours, but which also provides a system to work within. Unlike, say, a high-tech entrepreneur who must literally invent new ways of doing things, real estate entrepreneurs can put their own spin on well-established business models and take them to new heights.

GETTING STARTED

GETTING STARTED IS FAIRLY STRAIGHT forward. First, you have to decide to do it,

Many people think they would like to get into real estate. Most people never make the leap, however. Real estate requires an up-front investment for education, licensing and affiliation with a brokerage. There is no guarantee you will get any of your money back. For most people, real estate looks like a great way to make a living right up until the moment when they have to commit. If you really want to get into this business, the first thing you have to do is make the commitment and then follow through on it.

Once you have made the commitment you need a license. It is illegal to buy or sell real estate on behalf of paying clients without a license. The best way to earn a license is to start by enrolling in a course that meets the requirements of your state. In all states, agents must be at least 18 years old, complete a required course of study, and pass an exam. The biggest difference is in the number of hours of study required, which ranges from about 30 hours to 90 hours depending upon the state. Find an accredited course, pay the tuition and study hard. There is no guarantee you will pass the exam on the first try. Take your studies seriously.

Once you have a license, you will start your career by selling yourself. As an agent you will need to affiliate with an established brokerage. You will need to submit a résumé and sit for an interview. There are many books and websites with tips for interviewing success. Do everything you can to stand out from the crowd. If you are offered a position it will probably cost you some money to get started. Different brokerages have different rules, but you could find yourself paying fees to affiliate plus basic costs like printing business cards. Costs could be a few thousand dollars, not more.

ASOCIATIONS, PERIODICALS, WEBSITES

■ **American Real Estate and Urban Economics Association**
www.areuea.org

■ **American Society of Home Inspectors**
www.ashi.org

■ **Appraisal Institute**
www.appraisalinstitute.org

■ **Baird & Warner**
www.bairdwarner.com

■ **Century 21**
www.century21.com

■ **Certified Real Estate Agents**
www.crea.net

■ **Chandler Reports**
www.chandlerreports.com

■ **Coldwell Banker**
www.coldwellbanker.com

■ **Corcoran Group**
www.corcoran.com

■ **Crye-Leike**
www.crye-leike.com

■ **DePaul University**
www.depaul.edu

■ **ERA Realty**
www.era.com

■ **Institute of Real Estate Management**
www.irem.org

■ **Keller Williams**
www.kw.com

■ **Listing Book**
www.listingbook.com

■ **National Association of Home Inspectors**
www.nahi.org

■ **National Association of Independent Real Estate Brokers**
www.nationalrealestatebrokers.org

■ **National Association of Real Estate Brokers**
www.nareb.com

■ **National Association of Realtors**
www.realtor.org

■ **National Real Estate Investor**
www.nreionline.com

■ **National Real Estate Investors Association**
www.nationalreia.com

■ **Personal Real Estate Investor Magazine**
www.personalrealestateinvestormag.com

■ **Prudential Real Estate**
www.prudentialrealestate.com

■ **Real Estate Express**
www.realestateexpress.com

■ **Real Estate Library**
www.relibrary.com

■ **Re/Max**
www.remax.com

■ **Redfin**
www.redfin.com

■ **Sotheby's International Realty**
www.sothebysrealty.com

■ **Trulia**
www.trulia.com

■ **University of San Diego**
www.sandiego.com

■ **Zillow**
www.zillow.com

www.ingramcontent.com/pod-product-compliance
Lightning Source LLC
Chambersburg PA
CBHW070747180526
45168CB00004B/1562